S d

Angela Royston

D0178837

Raintree is an imprint of Capstone Global Library Limited, a company incorporated in England and Wales having its registered office at 264 Banbury Road, Oxford OX2 7DY – Registered company number: 6695582

www.raintree.co.uk
myorders@raintree.co.uk

Edited by Linda Staniford
Designed by Steve Mead
Picture research by Kelly Garvin
Production by Victoria Fitzgerald
Originated by Capstone Global Library Ltd
Printed and bound in China

ISBN 978 1 474 71422 8 (hardback)
19 18 17 16 15
10 9 8 7 6 5 4 3 2 1

ISBN 978 1 474 71428 0 (paperback)
20 19 18 17 16
10 9 8 7 6 5 4 3 2 1

British Library Cataloguing in Publication Data
A full catalogue record for this book is available from the British Library.

Acknowledgements
We would like to thank the following for permission to reproduce photographs:
Capstone Press/Karon Dubke, 8, 9, 16, 18, 19, 26, 27; Shutterstock: 3445128471, 7 (top left), absolute-india, 4, Alex Sun, 6, Amra Pasic, 15, cleanfotos, 5, Kzenon, 25, Liesel Fuchs, 20, Max Topchii, 17, Mr. Twister, 12, 23, Norman Chan, 21, Pavel L Photos and Video, 24, Reddogs, 7 (top right), Ronald Sumners, 13, steven r. hendricks, 22, tmcphotos, 11, Valua Vitaly, 10, Vinogradov Illya, cover, wavebreakmedia, 14, 29

We would like to thank Pat O'Mahony for his help in the preparation of this book.

Contents

Some words are shown in bold, **like this.** You can find out what they mean by looking in the glossary.

What is sound?

You hear sound when something, such as an object or the air, **vibrates**. This means that it trembles or shakes very fast. Loud sounds make stronger vibrations than quiet sounds.

The harder you clap your hands the louder the sound it makes.

The ambulance has a loud siren, which warns people to get out of the way.

If you listen carefully, you can probably hear several different sounds. Some sounds give information or warn of danger, but most sounds are made by people and things as they move.

Making sounds

There are many different ways to make sounds. Shakers contain small objects that rattle when the shaker is moved. You can also tap, rub or scrape one thing against another.

Scraping makes a different sound from tapping.

6

Humans and dogs make different sounds. Their sounds are made in the throat as they breathe out.

Machines and vehicles make a noise as their engines and other parts rattle and spin. You can often tell animals apart just by hearing the sounds they make.

Recognizing sounds

You will need:
- ✓ four empty plastic containers with tight lids
- ✓ a friend
- ✓ a blindfold
- ✓ a handful each of rice, pasta, sugar and marbles

1 Place the marbles in one container and put on the lid.

2 Do the same with each of the other substances.

3 Blindfold your friend. Choose one of the containers and shake it.

4 Can your friend guess what is inside?

5 Take turns to shake and to guess.

Check your results on page 28.

Musical sounds

Musical instruments include recorders, drums, violins, pianos and many others. Each instrument makes a different sound. The kind of sound it makes depends on its shape and how the sound is made.

You play a guitar by plucking the strings.

You blow into a recorder to make a sound.

Violins have strings, which are rubbed with a bow. A drum is tapped with a drumstick. **Wind instruments** such as trumpets and recorders make a sound when the player blows into them.

Sound waves

When something makes a sound, the vibrations make **sound waves**, which spread out in all directions.

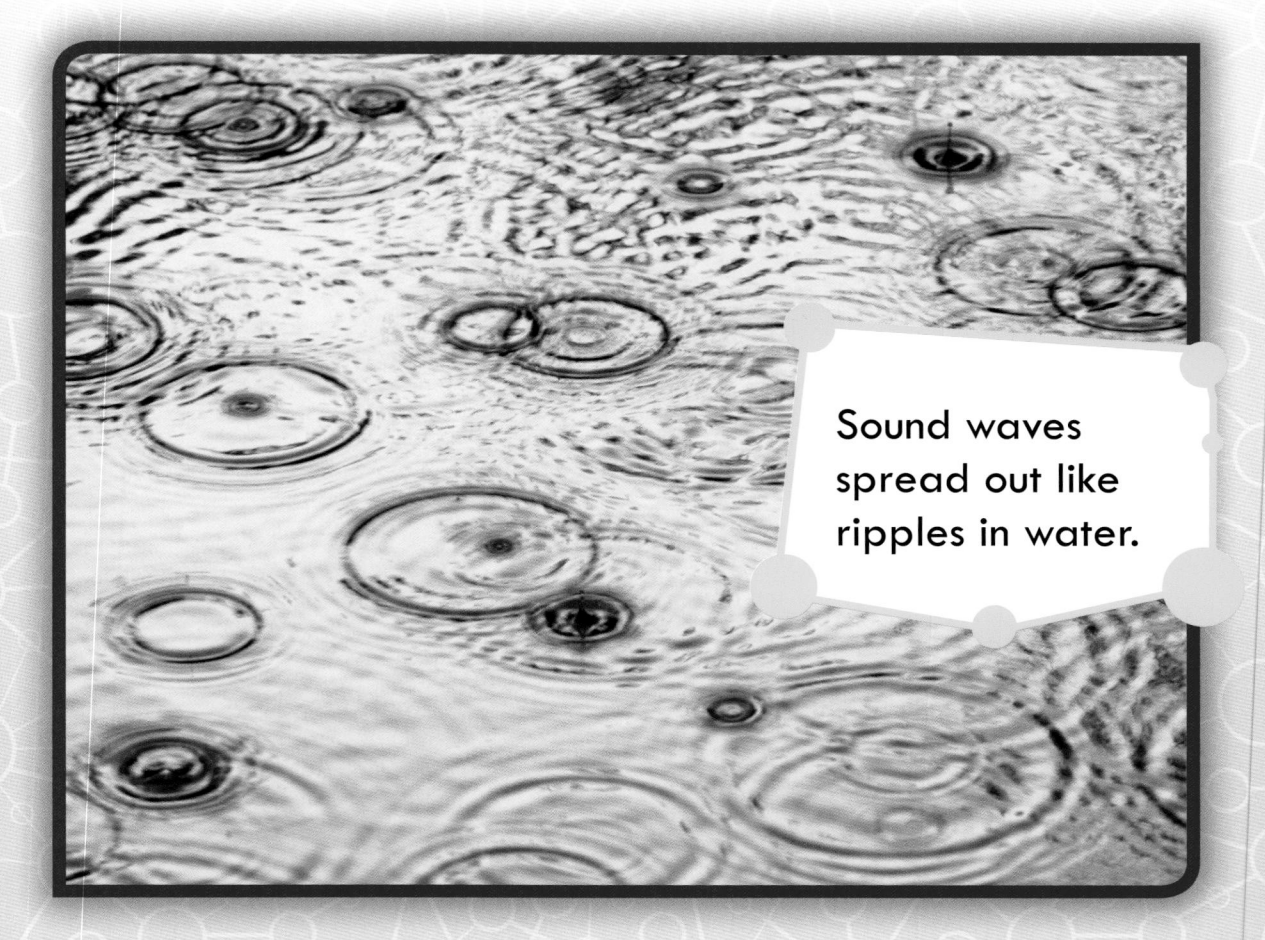

Sound waves spread out like ripples in water.

Sound waves in the air pass down the ear canal and deep into the ear.

Sound waves make anything they hit **vibrate** too. For example, you hear when sound waves move through the air and hit your eardrums. The closer you are to the sound, the louder it is.

Making sounds louder

Loud noises travel farther. A **megaphone** makes the human voice louder. It makes all the **sound waves** travel in the same direction instead of spreading out.

A megaphone is shaped like the end of a trumpet.

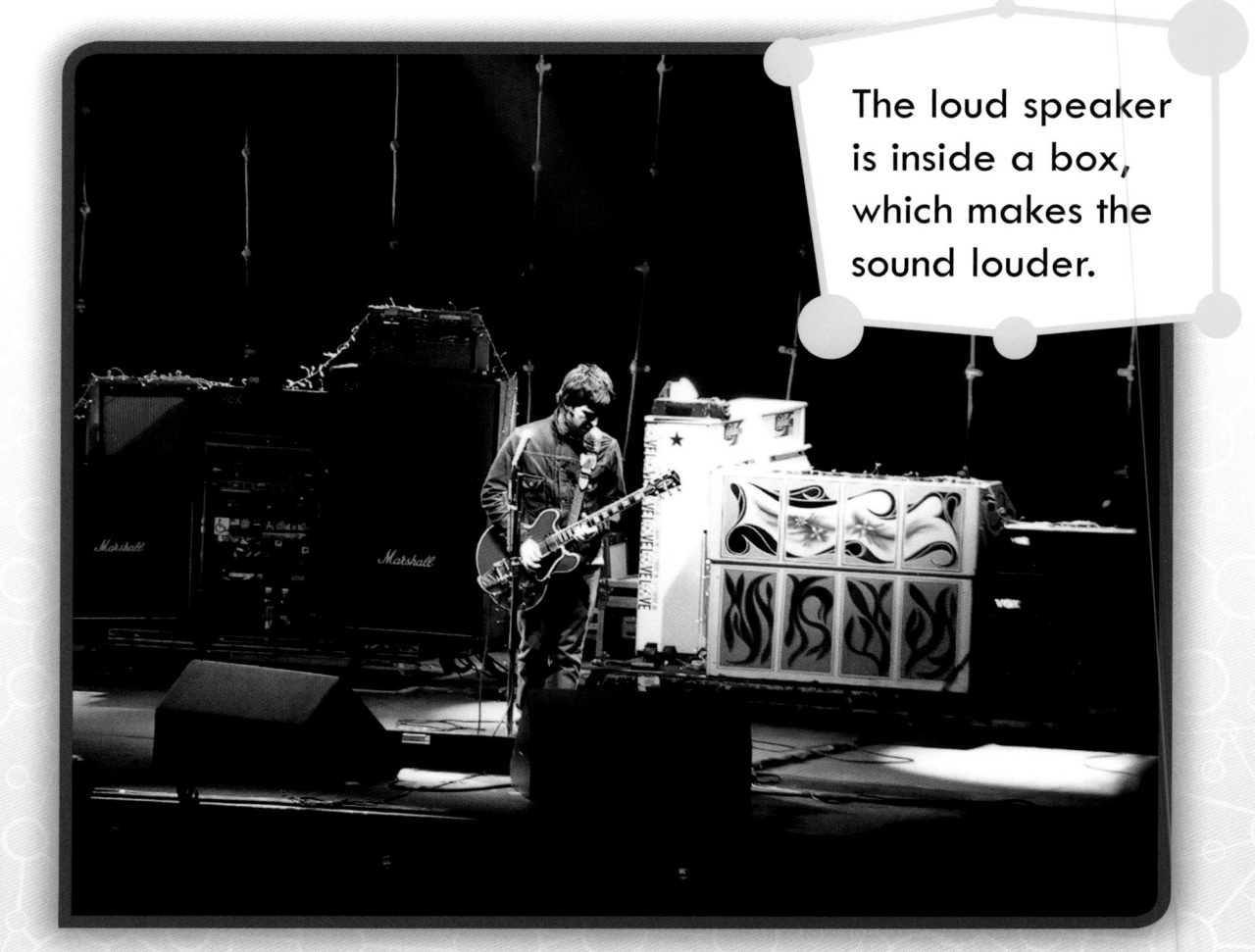

The loud speaker is inside a box, which makes the sound louder.

A loud speaker uses a type of megaphone to make **electronic** sounds louder. First it changes **electrical signals** into sound waves. Then it passes them through the megaphone.

Sound travels

Sound waves can travel through solids and liquids as well as through the air. You cannot see someone when they are in another room, but you can hear them. The sound waves travel through the wall.

If you knock on the wall the person in the next room will hear it.

You can hear sounds when your head is under water.

Sound travels farther through water than it does through air. The next time you are in a swimming pool, put your head under the water and listen.

Make a phone

You will need
- ✓ two empty plastic pots
- ✓ a piece of kite string or fishing line about 15 metres long
- ✓ a corkscrew
- ✓ a friend

1 Ask an adult to make a hole in the bottom of each pot with the corkscrew.

2 Push one end of the string through the hole into one pot and the other end through the hole into the other pot.

3 Knot the ends so they cannot slip out.

4 Stand far apart with the string tight. Listen to your end as your friend speaks into his or her end. Can you hear a voice?

Check your results on page 28.

High and low

Musical instruments do not just make sounds, they make musical notes. Each **key** of a xylophone plays a different **pitch**, or note, when it is tapped. Short keys make high notes and long keys make low notes.

With two sticks you can play two notes on a xylophone at the same time.

Each string on a harp plays a particular note.

A harp is played by plucking the strings. The strings are all different lengths and so play different notes. The short strings play higher notes than the longer strings.

Changing the note

Violins and cellos have only four strings but they can play many notes. The player presses her fingers on the strings to change their length. In this way she can play different notes.

A cello player plays higher notes by shortening the strings with her fingers.

Pressing a key on the trumpet changes the length of the column of air inside the tube.

When you blow into a **wind instrument**, the column of air inside **vibrates**. Changing the length of the column of air changes how high or low the note is.

Too much sound

Sound can sometimes be annoying. Materials, such as fibreglass, can be used to **absorb** the **sound waves** instead of passing them on. This is called sound-proofing.

The walls of this recording studio are covered with materials that absorb sound.

Earmuffs protect this worker's ears from the sound of the drill.

Very loud sounds can damage your ears. People who work around loud sounds wear earmuffs to protect their ears. The earmuffs stop most of the sound waves getting inside their ears.

Testing sound blockers

You will need

✓ a timer

✓ a large box

✓ materials such as bubble wrap, soft fabric, and crumpled newspaper – enough to fill the box with each

1 Pack the box with one of the materials.

2 Set the timer to 10 seconds and bury it inside the box. Put on the lid.

3 How close can you get to the box before you hear the timer?

4 Repeat with each of the materials.

5 Which material muffles the sound the best?

Check your results on page 28.

Experiment results
What happened?

Recognizing sounds (page 8)

You and your friend probably found some sounds, such as the marbles, easier to recognise than the others. Did you get better with practice?

Make a phone (page 18)

The **sound waves** made by your friend's voice should travel along the string to your end of the phone. If you cannot hear it, make sure that the string is tight.

Testing sound blockers (page 26)

Which material did you find worked best? You may have to listen carefully to detect the difference.

Quiz

1 The sound of a dog barking
   a gets louder as you move away
   b gets quieter as you move away
   c stays the same

2 A **megaphone** makes sound
   a louder
   b quieter
   c higher

3 On a harp, a short string
   a plays a lower note than a long string
   b plays the same note as a long string
   c plays a higher note than a long string

Turn to page 31 for the answers.

Glossary

absorb take in and hold

electrical signal information in a code created with electricity

electronic from a computer or other similar machine

key something tapped to make a musical note

megaphone machine that makes sound louder

pitch how high or low a sound is

sound wave change in the air or other materials that passes on sounds

vibrate shake very fast

wind instrument musical instrument that the player blows into to make sounds

Find out more

Books

Fizzing Physics (Science Crackers), Steve Parker (QED, 2012)

Light and Sound (Mind Webs), Anna Claybourne (Wayland 2014)

Sound (Moving up with Science), Peter Riley (Franklin Watts, 2015)

Websites

www.bbc.co.uk/bitesize/ks2/science/physical_processes/sound/read/1/

You'll find some good, clear information on this site, but the game is difficult!

www.sciencekids.co.nz/gamesactivities/changingsounds.html

Play the game to test how well you can detect pitch (how high or low a note is) and loudness.

Answers: 1b, 2a, 3c

Index